MIND
—THE—
GAP

21 BIBLICAL STEPS TO OVERCOMING NEGATIVE THOUGHTS AND RECLAIMING **A HEALTHY MIND**

ANDREW AND LESLEY CRISP

Table of Contents

Introduction

Three words printed on a sign outside a restaurant are intended to persuade dissatisfied customers to give it another try. Previously, the food had been bland, the staff were rude, and the tables were dirty. The establishment deserved its bad reputation. Now, however, there was good reason to believe it would be different.

The sign simply reads, "Under New Management."

The management had changed. And when the management changes, everything else can change.

When we become followers of Jesus, we bring our minds under new management—the Holy Spirit. That's great news because the Holy Spirit is a fantastic manager and changes the way we think.

"The mind governed by the Spirit is life and peace" (Romans 8:6).

Yet for many of us, the opposite is true. There is a gap between what the Bible promises and our daily experience. Instead of minds full of life and peace, we continue to experience negative thoughts—depression, anxiety, guilt, shame, self-rejection, failure, hurt, anger, bitterness, etc.

These thoughts crush our spirits, steal our joy, and stop us from enjoying God's life and peace.

In this book, you will learn to overcome negative thoughts and enjoy the healthy, vibrant Spirit-filled mind that God intends.

Before we begin, let's take some time to be still before God. Perhaps sit or kneel and pray along these lines:

Lord Jesus, thank you for your love and your desire to restore me. I submit my mind to You. I want Your Spirit to be in control of my mind, so that I overcome negative thoughts and experience life and peace instead. As I read this devotional, show me the steps I need to take to be free from negative thoughts and regain a healthy mind.

How to Make the Most of this Book

We all engage with God in different ways. We don't want to be too prescriptive, but we encourage everyone to consider these pointers.

Take it one step at a time.

You could probably finish this whole book in one day. Don't do that. You will get so much more out of the book if you take your time.

We recommend taking one step each day. Be still. Think about what you read. Pray.

Make unhurried space for God.

Christians often wonder how long they should pray. This question can sometimes lead to legalism.

Our priority should be to make unhurried space for God.

Go into a room by yourself Get rid of any distractions (including your phone). Close the door. Ask God to fill the space.

Whether you pray for a short time or a long time, don't rush. Give God time, and he will meet with you.

Begin with prayer.

Don't rush into reading each devotion. Before you read, ask the Holy Spirit to speak to you, encourage you, and show you what steps you need to take.

Have a Bible with you.

Each item in this devotional will include some Scripture references.

We would encourage you to look up the scriptures and spend time thinking about them. God will speak to you as you read and think about the scriptures.

Reflect and respond.

You'll experience the benefits of reading the devotional as you respond to God. Our goal is to point you to Him.

Each day, we will encourage you to respond in prayer. Sometimes this will be accompanied by:

- A time of silent reflection

- Kneeling or standing

- Writing your thoughts

Although we have written some suggested prayers, we hope you don't view these as a script. They're only examples of how you may want to pray. Talk to God in your own words.

Keep a journal.

A journal is a simple notebook in which you write:

- Thoughts you need to process

- Blessings you're thankful for

- Prayer requests

We make sense of what's going on in our minds and remember what God is doing for us by writing these down.

Some people draw pictures in their journals. Others may write poetry. Do what works for you.

Please give us feedback.

We'd love to hear your thoughts and reflections. When you've finished the book, please leave a helpful review on Amazon.

Or feel free to email us at:
feedback@andrewandlesley.org.

Think Differently

Gladys was confused.

She had been looking at the elephants next to the circus tent. These enormous animals were tied to a thin rope, which was attached to a small stake in the ground. They weren't in a cage, and they weren't chained up.

She asked a trainer, "These elephants are enormous! Why don't they just break away and go free?"

The trainer explained, "When the elephants are babies, they're much smaller and weaker. A tiny rope is enough to hold them. As they grow bigger and stronger, they believe they're still too weak to break the rope. They're conditioned to believe that they're trapped when they're not. As a result, they don't try to break free."

Gladys began to understand that the elephants were trapped—not by the rope but by their own thoughts.

When we come to Christ, we're set free from our past. But we're often so conditioned by our previous expectations that we don't enjoy that freedom. Instead, we continue living as we did before.

That's why the Bible tells us we need to change the way we think.

"Do not conform to the pattern of this world,
but be transformed by the renewing of your mind"
(Romans 12:2).

The truth sets us free, so if we feel bound up or held back, it's probably because we haven't grasped an aspect of God's truth. Our mindset holds us back because it's not consistent with what God says.

As our minds are renewed, we start to think in God's way. We see life and circumstances through a different lens. This new way of thinking is the foundation for a new way of living.

As you read this devotional, you'll get a clearer picture of God's love for you, your new identity in Christ, and the power of His Spirit inside you. The truth renews your mind and sets you free from wrong beliefs that have held you back.

Reflect and Respond

Father, thank you that I'm a new creation. The old has gone. The new has come. Forgive me that I've allowed my old mindsets to limit me and to stop me from becoming everything you intend me to be. I pray that you'll help me to identify the wrong ways of thinking. Help me to grasp the truth that sets me free.

Are there any old ways of thinking holding you back that you're aware of today? In your journal, write three mindsets that hold you back from experiencing freedom and joy in Christ.

As you read through this devotional, you will have the opportunity to discover other ways your mind needs to be renewed. Keep asking the Holy Spirit to reveal the truth you need to know.

Pulling Out the Weeds

This wasn't supposed to happen.

We'd finished the weeding, put the tools away, and everything looked beautiful.

But now, just two days later, the weeds were coming back! What had we done wrong?

Our mistake was obvious. We'd only broken off the visible parts of the weeds—the stalk and the leaves above the surface. The roots were still there, and so the weeds returned. Weeds need to be removed by the roots.

Jesus compares his heavenly Father to a gardener, determined to rid his garden of weeds. And he's not doing a quick fix. He's going beneath the surface, digging deep.

"Every plant that my heavenly father has not planted
will be pulled up by the roots"
(Matthew 15:13).

The weeds were the damaging teachings of the Pharisees—their judgmental attitudes, their lack of love, and their hypocrisy (see Matthew 15:1-9).

But if we're honest, we all have weeds in our lives—unwanted thoughts or actions that are causing damage and stopping us from being the fruitful people God intends. Sometimes those weeds are harmful to others. Often they only harm ourselves. Either way, they need to be removed.

When weeds spring up, the temptation is to deal with what we see on the surface. We may try to cancel painful thoughts with a quick fix. For some, that's alcohol, drugs, or pornography. For others, it may be more respectable distractions—entertainment, work, or busyness.

Not all these activities are wrong, but if we use them to block out negative emotions, we miss out on the deeper work God wants to do. Life may feel better for a while, but if the root remains, the weeds will return.

That's why God lovingly uproots harmful thought patterns. In their place, he plants new ways of thinking based on truth.

Invite God into the garden of your mind. Trust him to uproot everything he hasn't planted.

Reflect and Respond

The Bible often compares God to a gardener. He planted a garden in Eden (Genesis 2:8). In Isaiah 5, God established a vineyard on a fertile hillside—a metaphor for Israel and the good things he has done for them. In John 15, he's the vinedresser, faithfully pruning us to bear fruit. Spend some time thinking about God as a gardener in your life.

Father God, thank you that you lovingly uproot everything in my mind that you haven't planted. Forgive me that at times, I've tried to cancel negative thoughts with easy distractions, such as [name anything you're aware of]. I ask you to dig deep into my mind. As I read through this devotional, make me aware of any thought patterns that shouldn't be there. I ask you to dig them up by the roots and plant new ways of thinking instead.

Write down any weeds you've become aware of today. Ask God to pull them up by the roots and plant new ways of thinking instead.

Day 3

Chewing over God's Word

Have you ever watched a cow eating grass?

When cows first take a bite of grass, they chew it very little before swallowing. But later, they lie down and "un-swallow" the grass—they bring it back into their mouths. Then they chew the same grass again. Then swallow again. This process is known as chewing the cud.

Cows can spend hours each day chewing the cud. By thoroughly grinding the grass, their bodies digest the food and absorb its nutrients more effectively.

This image illustrates how and why we meditate on Scripture. We chew it in our minds. That helps us digest God's truth and absorb its goodness fully.

"May these words of my mouth and this meditation of my heart be pleasing in your sight, Lord, my Rock and my Redeemer" (Psalm 19:14).

If we think carefully about Scripture, the truth nourishes us and lives in us.

"Let the message of Christ dwell in you richly"
(Colossians 3:16).

Our minds often benefit more from focusing on a small passage than a large chunk of the Bible. The British preacher Charles Spurgeon expressed it like this: "I would rather lay my soul asoak in half a dozen verses all day than rinse my hand in several chapters. Oh, to be bathed in a text of Scripture, and to let it be sucked up in your very soul, till it saturates your heart!"

Many people unintentionally meditate on negative thoughts. They think over their hurts, regrets, and disappointments. Sometimes that causes depression or other mental illnesses.

But there's an alternative. We can choose what to think about.

"Whatever is true, whatever is noble, whatever is right, whatever is pure, whatever is lovely, whatever is admirable—if anything is excellent or praiseworthy—think about such things"
(Philippians 4:8).

As you read through this devotional, there will be moments when you become aware of negative thoughts. Meditating on the Scriptures will help you to replace damaging mindsets with upbuilding thoughts.

God's Word comes to dwell in us as we allow his truth to renew our minds. It's the most nourishing food we'll ever eat.

Reflect and Respond

What helps you to meditate on God's Word?

There are many ways to meditate. Try these simple steps:

1. Go to a quiet place alone.

2. Ask the Holy Spirit to speak to you as you meditate.

3. Read a scripture, such as Psalm 18:1-3, out loud.

4. Think about what it means.

5. Reread it silently.

6. Thank God for each truth in those verses. For example, *"Thank you, God, that you are my rock."*

7. Pause between each thank you prayer and imagine what that looks like. For example, what does it mean for God to be your rock?

8. Sit in silence and write down anything you feel God may be saying to you.

9. Perhaps return to the same scripture later in the day, recalling it before you eat or go to bed.

As you continue through this devotional, you may want to meditate on some of the scriptures mentioned.

Singing God's Word is also a form of meditation—has God put a song on your heart? Allow it to revolve around your mind.

Drink Deeply

Steve had been walking for several miles in the heat of the day. His feet were tired, sweat was dripping down his forehead, and he was desperate for a drink.

He walked into a café, sat down, and asked the waiter for a glass of water.

"Certainly, sir," the waiter replied, "Here's a book."

"What's this?" asked Steve.

"It's a book about water," explained the waiter.

Steve was confused. "I don't need a book about water. I need water."

"Oh, I see," said the waiter. "Perhaps you'd like to join us at the table over there. We're going to be discussing water."

"No," said Steve. "I don't want to *discuss* water. I need to *drink* water."

"I understand," said the waiter. "I'll go and get my guitar." The waiter began to walk off.

"Where are you going?" asked Steve.

"I'm going to get my guitar so we can sing some songs about water."

Steve walked out of the café, still thirsty.

This modern-day parable makes an important point about our deepest need. We don't just need a book about God. We need God himself. Jesus promised that there's a real spiritual drink for his followers to receive.

"On the last and greatest day of the festival, Jesus stood and said in a loud voice, 'Let anyone who is thirsty come to me and drink. Whoever believes in me, as Scripture has said, rivers of living water will flow from within them.' By this he meant the Spirit, whom those who believed in him were later to receive" (John 7:37-39a).

Throughout this devotional are scriptures to read each day. But intellectual knowledge of Scripture isn't enough to renew our minds. We need the Holy Spirit. He enables us to understand in our hearts the scriptures we know in our minds. The Holy Spirit gives us revelation—not just information.

"What we have received is not the spirit of the world, but the Spirit who is from God, so that we may understand what God has freely given us" (1 Corinthians 2:12).

Knowledge of the Bible on its own won't bring us a healthy relationship with God. The Holy Spirit helps us to know God as our Father and to find security in our new identity as his children.

"The Spirit you received does not make you slaves, so that you live in fear again; rather, the Spirit you received brought about your adoption to sonship. And by him we cry, 'Abba, Father.' The Spirit himself testifies with our spirit that we are God's children" (Romans 8:15-16).

The Holy Spirit wants to speak to you through the Scriptures. Don't settle for a head full of Bible knowledge—God has much more for you than that. Make it a priority to drink in the Holy Spirit and know God personally.

Reflect and Respond

A crucial step to being filled with the Holy Spirit is to ask. Jesus promised that the Father would give the Holy Spirit to everyone who asks (Luke 11:9-13). Perhaps pray a prayer like this:

Father God, Jesus promised that you would give the Holy Spirit to everyone who asks you. I acknowledge my need for the Holy Spirit. I cannot fully grasp the truth about your love and my new identity without the revelation that comes from your Spirit. Please fill me today and every day. Let your Holy Spirit bring the Scriptures to light and enable me to understand who you are and all that you have given me.

You may find it helpful to ask a friend to pray with you. Often, people receive the Holy Spirit when others lay hands on them (Acts 8:17).

Cast All Your Anxiety onto Him

How do you respond to anxiety?

A charity shop in King's Lynn, England, sells a variety of secondhand goods. But there's one item that's not for sale—a simple wooden-back green armchair.

"It is a worry chair," explained the shop owner. "Anyone who sits in that chair will be brought tea and biscuits. We try to take people's worries away. Sometimes it can take a couple of times before they open up and get used to us, and we can help them with whatever they are worried about."[1]

We all need somewhere to go with our anxieties. When Peter wrote to persecuted Christians, he knew they'd have plenty to worry about—losing their homes or experiencing violence or even death. How should they respond?

Peter didn't direct them to a worry chair. He pointed them to God.

> "Humble yourselves, therefore, under God's mighty hand,
> that he may lift you up in due time.
> Cast all your anxiety on him because he cares for you"
> (1 Peter 5:6-7).

What does it mean to cast our anxiety on God? To cast means to throw upon or simply to place upon. The Bible uses the same Greek word when the disciples "threw" their cloaks onto a colt (Luke 19:35). We can throw our anxiety onto Jesus, and he carries it. Our problems may remain, but Jesus bears the weight. Our anxieties need not weigh us down.

Peter didn't promise the things they were worried about wouldn't happen. The church was suffering all kinds of pain and loss. He wasn't giving them a formula for an easy life. The Bible does, however, promise that we don't go through these things alone. Jesus is with us. He understands. He gives us strength.

> "Cast your cares on the Lord and he will sustain you"
> (Psalm 55:22).

"Praise be to the Lord, to God our Saviour,
who daily bears our burdens"
(Psalm 68:19*)*.

We all experience anxiety, but we don't need to be worn out by it. The Lord will bear our burdens and sustain us. Jesus cares for each of us.

Reflect and Respond

In what ways does anxiety affect your life?

Try this simple exercise as a way of casting your cares onto Jesus.

Kneel before God quietly as an outward sign of your humility and trust in him. Begin to acknowledge his greatness and his blessings in your life.

Hold out your hands, palms upwards, and imagine your anxieties resting in your hands. Name those anxieties before God.

Now turn your hands over, palms downwards, and imagine your anxieties falling into the hands of Jesus, as you pray, "*Lord Jesus, I cast my anxiety onto you. Thank you that you care for me.*"

Peace Beyond Understanding

The U.S. Navy was testing a submarine. It had to be submerged deep under the ocean from evening until morning. During the night, there was a violent thunderstorm with torrential rain, dangerous winds, and pounding waves.

The following morning, the submarine returned to the surface. "How did you cope with the storm last night?" asked an anxious officer.

The captain looked at him in surprise. "What storm?" he asked.

The storm had been fierce, but the submarine was so deep in the ocean, it was unaffected.

In the book of Philippians, the apostle Paul was surrounded by storms. The Romans had arrested him and chained him up (Philippians 1:13). Preachers with dubious motives were stirring up trouble (1:15-17). He didn't even know if he would live or die (1:20).

Yet Paul was seemingly unaffected. He was so deep in Christ that he could enjoy peace amid trouble. And he tells the church how they can experience the same.

"Do not be anxious about anything, but in every situation, by prayer and petition, with thanksgiving, present your requests to God. And the peace of God, which transcends all understanding, will guard your hearts and your minds in Christ Jesus"
(Philippians 4:6-7).

By bringing thankful prayers to God in every situation, we can experience a supernatural peace that is not dependent on our circumstances.

It was the same security God had promised through Isaiah:

"You will keep in perfect peace those whose minds are steadfast, because they trust in you"
(Isaiah 26:3).

Your circumstances don't have to steal your peace. If you're going through storms, let them remind you to go deeper into Christ. Take your anxious thoughts to him. Your problems may remain, but God's perfect peace will guard your heart and mind.

Reflect and Respond

What are you anxious about most often?

Thank you, God, that you promise peace in every situation. Thank you that your peace guards my heart and mind. Forgive me for the times I've allowed anxiety to steal that peace. I pray that you'll teach me to live deeply in Christ and enjoy your peace more fully.

Some Christian traditions find it helpful to do a breathing exercise. As you breathe out, imagine breathing out your anxieties. As you breathe in, imagine receiving the peace of God.

Don't Give the Devil a Foothold

Have you ever tried to climb a smooth wall?

If you're a rock climber, you'll know you need somewhere to put your feet, a piece of rock where you can stand while you plan your next move.

It's known as a foothold—a place where the climber can lodge their foot, a secure position from which they can make further progress.

The devil looks for a foothold in our lives—a place where he can stand so that he can make further progress. Paul told the Ephesians that they were giving the devil a foothold by not resolving their anger.

> "In your anger do not sin: Do not let the sun go down while you are still angry, and do not give the devil a foothold" (Ephesians 4:26-27).

Anger isn't always wrong. Even Jesus got angry (Mark 3:5). But if we don't resolve the anger quickly, it becomes toxic. Unresolved anger ruins friendships and even marriages, as well as causing both mental and physical illness.

We can't resolve these issues unless we first let go of anger and forgive those who have hurt us.

Forgiveness is a spiritual issue. It's a crucial step to overcoming Satan's schemes:

"Anyone you forgive, I also forgive. And what I have forgiven—if there was anything to forgive—I have forgiven in the sight of Christ for your sake, in order that Satan might not outwit us. For we are not unaware of his schemes"
(2 Corinthians 2:10-11).

When we forgive, the foothold crumbles, and the devil has nowhere to stand. He can't continue his progress in our lives.

As Lewis B. Smedes said[2]: "To forgive is to set a prisoner free and discover that the prisoner was you."

Don't give the devil a foothold in your life. Let go of your anger. Forgive those who have hurt you, and enjoy the peace that God has for you.

Reflect and Respond

Write down on some scrap paper the names of any people, organisations, or situations that have caused you anger. Ask the Holy Spirit to help you to forgive.

When you're ready, throw the paper away as a way of demonstrating your decision not to hold on to that anger.

You may find a prayer like this helpful:

Father, forgive me for holding on to bitterness and judgments. I release [name] from my judgment, and I forgive them for [how they sinned against me—you may want to be specific]. I commit them to you. I pray that you will do them good. I forgive them in the sight of Christ. I let go of all bitterness and anger. Instead, I receive peace, joy, and freedom.

A Safe Way to Deal with Anger

Lightning is a destructive force.

A typical lightning flash is 300 million volts. That's enough to power a light bulb for six months. The air around the lightning bolt is three times hotter than the surface of the sun. No wonder lightning destroys so many buildings.

But there is a way to manage it safely. The Empire State Building in New York is struck by lightning about twenty-five times each year. Yet it experiences little or no damage. Why? It's protected by a lightning rod.

A copper rod placed at the top of a building is connected to a grid of wires that runs down to a ground rod and safely disperses the electrical current. The destructive force is made safe because it's properly managed.

Anger is also a destructive force. It causes all kinds of damaging behaviour—malicious talk, vengefulness, and murder.

> "Human anger does not produce
> the righteousness that God desires"
> (James 1:20).

Even if we don't commit these outward sins, anger can burn in us, making us bitter, resentful, and depressed. All this grieves the Holy Spirit.

"And do not grieve the Holy Spirit of God, with whom you were sealed for the day of redemption. Get rid of all bitterness, rage and anger, brawling and slander, along with every form of malice. Be kind and compassionate to one another, forgiving each other, just as in Christ God forgave you"
(Ephesians 4:30-32).

We need a lightning rod for our anger.

God is that lightning rod. He can deal with our anger. We can tell Him everything we're feeling and express our pain and sense of injustice to Him. We can release all our emotions onto Him, even if we're unreasonable.

We may even be angry at God. Jeremiah wasn't afraid to say that he felt God had tricked him:

"You deceived me, Lord, and I was deceived; you overpowered me and prevailed. I am ridiculed all day long; everyone mocks me" (Jeremiah 20:7).

God is not a deceiver. But that's how Jeremiah felt, so that's what he said.

If we unleash our anger on others, it causes damage. If we bottle it up, we get depressed. Unresolved anger harms ourselves and other people.

Be completely honest with God, and don't hold back. Tell Him everything in your own unfiltered words. Get everything out of your heart and onto Him. Let God be your lightning rod.

Reflect and Respond

Who or what are you angry with?

Find a place where you can pray out loud without anyone hearing you. Perhaps that's your home when everyone else is out? Or maybe you need to go for a walk on your own somewhere?

Tell God everything in your own words. Whatever you're feeling, tell Him. Keep going until you feel you've released all your anger to Him.

Gaining Perspective

A mischievous student has won a prize for a school project titled "How Gullible Are People?"

He persuaded fifty people to sign a petition urging the government to ban water. Without telling anyone he was referring to water, he focused people's minds only on its negative aspects.

"It causes soil erosion," he told them. "It causes hundreds of deaths every year. It's one of the main ingredients in acid rain. Many athletes use it as a performance enhancer."

People were so horrified that the government was doing nothing about it that they signed the petition, demanding that this destructive substance be banned.

This story demonstrates that when people focus entirely on negative things, they reach ridiculous conclusions. We can sometimes do that when we look at ourselves.

If we focus on the negative aspects of our lives, we experience thoughts like:

- Everything is hopeless.

- My life is ruined.

- I can never be happy.

We may even conclude that the world would be a better place without us. These thoughts are not consistent with how God sees us.

We need to stop focusing on the negative and instead learn thankfulness for the many blessings in our lives.

The apostle Paul knew much pain in his life—disappointments, rejection, betrayal, persecution—yet he remained thankful. And that was the attitude he urged his fellow Christians to have.

"Rejoice always, pray continually, give thanks in all circumstances; for this is God's will for you in Christ Jesus" (1 Thessalonians 5:16-18).

Regular thanksgiving is one of the most effective steps to increasing our happiness and reducing depression. Expressing gratitude reduces toxic emotions, such as envy, resentment, and regret.

Thankfulness reminds us of what he has done in the past and builds our faith for the future.

"Count your blessings, name them one by one;

Count your blessings, see what God has done;

Count your blessings, name them one by one,

And it will surprise you what the Lord has done."[3]

Be intentional about finding things to thank God for, whatever your circumstances. You may be surprised to find that God's goodness has impacted your life in far more ways than you realised.

Reflect and Respond

Father God, thank you for the many blessings in my life. Forgive me for the times I've been complaining and ungrateful. Would you please help me to see more clearly the gifts that you've given me?

How often do you thank God?

A great way to remember God's blessings is to keep a record of what you're thankful for in a journal. Take time each day to write down some things you're grateful for. You may want to try writing ten each day. In one hundred days, you will have thanked God for one thousand blessings.

Learning Contentment

Bigger. Better. Faster. More.

When the British band, Four Non-Blondes, chose those words as the title for their first album, they summed up a typical attitude that affects us all.

There's a feeling we'll all be happier if we could just have . . . a bigger house? a better phone? a faster car? More money?

What is it for you?

When we have the mindset of "I'll be happy when . . . ," we're missing out on the freedom of contentment.

Jesus saw through the folly of this thinking. He didn't have much of what the world values highly—he wasn't rich, he wasn't married, and he wasn't popular much of the time. Yet he had a life of joy and contentment that attracted many to follow him. He taught his disciples:

"Life does not consist in an abundance of possessions"
(Luke 12:15).

The apostle Paul discovered this for himself. After losing everything as he followed God's call, he knew a richness in his soul that many long for. He described himself as "Having nothing, and yet possessing everything" (2 Corinthians 6:10).

Despite his trials, his mind was at peace. He testified:

"I have learned to be content whatever the circumstances. I know what it is to be in need, and I know what it is to have plenty. I have learned the secret of being content in any and every situation, whether well fed or hungry,
whether living in plenty or in want.
I can do all this through him who gives me strength"
(Philippians 4:11-13).

Let's learn to enjoy each day, appreciate what we have, and discover that we are complete in Jesus. That is true contentment.

Reflect and Respond

To what extent are you content?

Today, make a special effort to enjoy every moment. Appreciate each person you meet. Thank God for all you have.

Father, thank you for all that you've given me [name some example]. Thank you that I can find contentment in knowing you. Forgive me for the times I have looked to other things to meet my need [name them]. Teach me to be content in any and every situation.

Fight the FOMO

Do you ever feel like other people are having a better time than you?

In the early 2000s, students at Harvard Business School identified a social anxiety called "FOMO"—the Fear Of Missing Out. Researchers defined FOMO as a "pervasive apprehension that others might be having rewarding experiences from which one is absent."[4]

With the rise of social media, other people's lives are on display like never before—holidays, parties, festivals, weddings, successful careers. It may feel like everyone is having an exciting life except us. Seeing everyone else's happy lives can lead to unhealthy emotions, like jealousy, self-pity, or feeling left out. FOMO steals our contentment and peace.

But FOMO is nothing new. It's as old as the earth itself. Why was Eve so easily deceived by the serpent? Perhaps she was afraid of missing out. She began to believe that there were benefits to eating the fruit that she would miss out on if she listened to God.

"'You will not certainly die,' the serpent said to the woman. 'For God knows that when you eat from it your eyes will be opened, and you will be like God, knowing good and evil.'

"When the woman saw that the fruit of the tree was good for food and pleasing to the eye, and also desirable for gaining wisdom, she took some and ate it" (Genesis 3:4-6a).

Eve's experience has been repeated throughout history—doubting God's goodness and the temptation to choose what may appear to be a more appealing option. Even Peter had to learn to be content with God's path for his life. When he learned that following Jesus would one day cost him his life, he looked over his shoulder and saw John.

"Peter turned and saw that the disciple whom Jesus loved was following them . . . When Peter saw him, he asked, 'Lord, what about him?'

"Jesus answered, 'If I want him to remain alive until I return, what is that to you? You must follow me'" (John 21:20-22).

Peter questioned whether John would also die for his faith. Jesus gently told him that his plan for John was none of Peter's business. Peter's priority must be to follow Jesus wherever that took him.

One of the first steps to overcoming FOMO is to accept that we can't experience everything. Missing out is inevitable. Comparing ourselves to others distracts us from God's call on our lives.

So think about your life and appreciate what you *have*— not what you *don't have*. God's greatest gift to us is himself. By learning to be satisfied with God and the blessings he chooses to give, you'll be able to say with King David, "LORD, you alone are my portion and my cup; you make my lot secure. The boundary lines have fallen for me in pleasant places; surely I have a delightful inheritance" (Psalm 16:5-6).

Reflect and Respond

In what ways do you feel you're missing out? Express those feelings to God in prayer.

Take a fresh look at your life and continue to thank God for his blessings, both big and small.

Thank you, God, for all your blessing in my life and the lives of others. Forgive me that I don't always appreciate your many blessings. Help me to always be mindful of your presence.

Day 12

Whose Words Define You?

"Let her die."

Rose's grandfather saw her as worthless. Born three months premature in a culture that preferred boys, an incubator was keeping her alive. She wasn't worth saving.

Her parents disagreed and urged the doctors to persevere. Rose survived and left the hospital two months later.

But her grandfather despised her. As she grew up, he told her she was worthless and would never amount to anything. He bought presents for her siblings but not for her. She felt hurt and rejected.

Determined to prove herself, she studied hard at school. She was at the top of her class, and a top school awarded her a scholarship. Her teachers and parents were delighted, but her grandfather continued to criticise her. Despite all her achievements, she felt rejected and inferior.

Rose's story reminds us that harsh words from close family members can cause as much damage as a physical weapon.

"The words of the reckless pierce like swords"
(Proverbs 12:18).

Even when they're entirely untrue, people's words can crush us.

"A deceitful tongue crushes the spirit"
(Proverbs 15:4, NLT).

If we're not careful, we can feel condemned, ashamed, and worthless when we have no reason to. You may have been told hurtful things like

- You're hopeless.

- You'll never amount to anything.

- It's all your fault.

- What's wrong with you?

- Why can't you be more like your cousin?

But those words don't have to define you because they aren't what God thinks of you. God is your Father, and his view is more important than anyone else's.

Rose learnt this for herself at age sixteen. A Christian teacher told her that she was great—not because of academic success, but because God had created her.

Rose never forgot what the teacher said, and she began to see herself differently. Three months later, Rose became a Christian and began learning the full extent of God's love for her. Each morning, she looked in the mirror and said, "You are loved and accepted."

She forgave her grandfather and found peace in knowing God accepts her for who she is.

She now serves God as a missionary, spreading the message of God's unconditional love around the world.

Reflect and Respond

What is the most hurtful thing anyone ever said about you? Has it shaped how you view yourself?

What does God say about that? Ask the Holy Spirit to reveal the truth that will set you free. You *may want to pray along the following lines:*

Father God, I forgive [name] for telling me [...........]. I recognise that those words are not from you. Sorry that I've allowed those words to shape me and cause me to think negatively about myself. I break the power of those words in Jesus' name.

Some find it helpful to speak out faith statements based on the promises of Scripture. For example:

"*I am wonderfully made*" (Psalm 139:14).

"*Jesus loves me and gave himself for me*" (Galatians 2:20).

"*I am forgiven and clean*" (1 John 1:9).

"*I am a new creation. The old has gone. The new has come*" (2 Corinthians 5:17).

"*I am a child of God*" (Romans 8:16).

Day 13

Anointed and Depressed

"Why am I like this?"

Dave had been a missionary for fifteen years, sharing the gospel and providing practical help in over twenty countries. He loved God and enjoyed a close walk with him.

But after becoming the victim of a horrific crime, his mental health deteriorated. He questioned why God had allowed it to happen. He lost all motivation, questioning whether he could keep serving God or how he could even continue with life.

Is it normal for Christians to feel like that?

It may surprise you that some of the leading figures in the Bible experienced depression. Elijah was righteous, anointed, and full of faith. Yet the Bible tells us:

"He came to a broom bush, sat down under it and prayed that he
might die. 'I have had enough, Lord,' he said.
'Take my life; I am no better than my ancestors'"
(1 Kings 19:4).

Jonah also wanted to die.

"Now, Lord, take away my life, for it is better for me to die
than to live . . . And I'm so angry I wish I were dead"
(Jonah 4:3, 9).

Jeremiah wished he'd never been born.

"Cursed be the day I was born! Why did I ever come out of the
womb to see trouble and sorrow and to end my days in shame?"
(Jeremiah 20:14, 18).

Even mature Christians can sometimes feel life is so
terrible that they can't go on. The apostle Paul was not
ashamed to admit his trials were so great that he questioned
whether he wanted to go on living.

"We were under great pressure, far beyond our ability to endure,
so that we despaired of life itself"
(2 Corinthians 1:8).

God helps different people in different ways. Elijah
needed rest and food, as well as perspective and fresh vision.
Jonah needed to learn to be more gracious. Jeremiah needed

to rant at God. Paul found comfort in God's deliverance and the prayers of his fellow Christians.

Do you ever feel depressed? Find comfort in knowing you're not alone. There isn't always a simple solution but, in God, there is hope.

Dave's depression lasted for two years, but he found healing by God's grace and the help of friends. He forgave the perpetrator of the crime, he regained perspective, and he continues to serve God. To his amazement, he discovered that God is using his experience to help him support others in their pain.

Reflect and Respond

In what ways have you experienced depression?

Invite God into your depression. Perhaps pray something like this:

Father, I thank you that you are close to the brokenhearted. You are the light that shines in my darkness. You see my depression, and you know the cause. I bring it to you and pray that you will bring me healing in whatever way you choose. I put my hope in you.

Day 14

Preach the Gospel to Yourself

"Come on! You can do this. Concentrate."

Many sports players use self-talk to improve their game. By sending themselves positive messages, they regain their focus, increase their motivation, and achieve the right frame of mind for victory.

Modern business coaches have also recognised the importance of talking to yourself to improve confidence and achieve commercial success.

Yet self-talk is nothing new. The psalm writers, such as King David, talked to themselves. In Psalms 42 and 43, the psalmist challenges himself with a question.

"Why, my soul, are you downcast? Why so disturbed within me?"
(Psalm 42:5a).

When he says "my soul," he is addressing himself. The word *downcast* means despairing, bowed down, or depressed. He is asking himself why he feels depressed.

He then tells himself what to do.

> "Put your hope in God, for I will yet praise him,
> my Saviour and my God"
> (Psalm 42:5b).

He urges his soul to look to God again. He reminds himself who God is. He is stirring himself to praise God, even though he doesn't feel like it.

In other psalms, we see the writer urging himself to praise God and remember what God has done.

> "Praise the Lord, my soul; all my inmost being, praise his holy name. Praise the Lord, my soul, and forget not all his benefits" (Psalm 103:1-2).

Self-talk can work the other way, too. We can end up crushing ourselves with words like:

- Why am I such an idiot?

- I'm such a failure.

- I may as well give up.

In his book, *Spiritual Depression*, Martin Lloyd Jones writes: "The main trouble in this whole matter of spiritual depression in a sense is this, that we allow our self to talk to us instead of talking to our self. Have you realised that most of your unhappiness in life is due to the fact that you are listening to yourself instead of talking to yourself?" [5]

In seasons of barrenness and disappointment, how do you respond? Perhaps you begin to lose faith in the goodness of God? Or do you question whether God is really with you?

If you feel despair, disappointment, or loneliness, talk to yourself. Preach the gospel to yourself. Remind yourself of all that God has done. As you do that, you'll find your spirit is once again released in praise to God.

Reflect and Respond

Read Psalms 42 and 43. In what ways do you relate to the experiences described in those psalms?

It might seem a bit strange at first, but try preaching some scriptures to yourself. Remind yourself of who you are and who God is.

Why are you downcast, [insert your name]? Why are you depressed and anxious? Put your trust in God. He is your rock. He is your fortress. He is your safe stronghold. Nothing can separate you from his love. God did not spare His only son but gave Him up for you. Will He not graciously, along with him, give you all things? God is for you. Who can be against you? Nothing can separate you from his love. Put your trust in Him. He is your Saviour. He is your God.

Day 15

A Different Type of Warfare

In February 1942, while the world was being torn apart by the Second World War, C. S. Lewis wrote a novel about a different type of warfare.

The Screwtape Letters[6] is a series of imagined letters between a senior demon, Screwtape, and his nephew, Wormwood. Screwtape is teaching Wormwood how to tempt a Christian away from God's path.

When C. S. Lewis was asked whether he really believed in the devil, he responded:

"If by 'the devil' you mean a power opposite to God, the answer is certainly no. God has no opposite. The proper question is whether I believe in the devils. I do. That is to say, I believe in angels, and I believe that some of these . . . have become enemies of God. Satan, the leader or dictator of devils, is the opposite, not of God, but of [the Archangel] Michael."[7]

Whilst *The Screwtape Letters* is intended to be a lighthearted look at the battles Christians face, it's also a reminder that the spiritual realm is real.

"For our struggle is not against flesh and blood, but against the rulers, against the authorities, against the powers of this dark world and against the spiritual forces of evil in the heavenly realms" (Ephesians 6:12).

Many paintings or Hollywood movies depict the devil with bright red horns, a forked tail, and a pitchfork. If someone like that knocked at your door, you wouldn't let him in! But he's much more subtle than that.

The emphasis of the Bible's teaching about the devil is not on his strength or power. It's his schemes (Ephesians 6:11), cunning (2 Corinthians 11:3), and deceit (Revelation 20:8).

We need to be discerning. We can't blame everything on the devil. Jesus said evil thoughts come out of our own hearts (Matthew 15:19). We must take responsibility for these and repent of them.

Our upbringing or cultural expectations also affect how we think. We need our minds to be renewed if that influence is not consistent with God's values.

In some cases, poor mental health may require professional help. God often uses medical professionals and medication to help us.

But many of our destructive thought patterns have a spiritual source. We need to keep a healthy balance. As C. S. Lewis said: "There are two equal and opposite errors into which our race can fall about the devils. One is to disbelieve in their existence. The other is to believe, and to feel an excessive and unhealthy interest in them."[8]

Reflect and Respond

How aware are you of the spiritual realm?

Ask for the Holy Spirit's help in discerning whether some of your negative thoughts have a spiritual root. Stand and pray against these thoughts in Jesus' name.

Father, thank you that your Spirit in me is greater than any other spiritual power. Forgive me for the times I've listened to the devil's lies. Open my eyes to the spiritual realm and how it affects me. Please give me discernment to understand when the devil is influencing my thoughts. Teach me how to overcome.

Don't Be Deceived

The vine snake is a master of disguise.

Hiding in the rainforests of Asia, this slender green serpent feeds on frogs and lizards. Although it's mostly harmless to humans, it's rumoured to be able to blind people. The scientific name for the snake, "Ahaetulla," means "eye plucker."

What is its secret weapon? How does it capture its prey so successfully? By using camouflage. It looks like a beautiful, harmless vine when in fact it's violent and deadly.

Jesus told his disciples that he is "the true vine" (John 15:1). But there is also a false vine, pretending to be the true vine to mislead Jesus' disciples. The apostle Paul warned the Corinthian church:

> "Satan himself masquerades as an angel of light"
> (2 Corinthians 11:14).

The devil tries to mislead us by whispering thoughts into our minds—not just blatant lies but also half-truths, exaggerations, and misused Scriptures. These whispers may seem like our own thoughts or even the voice of God—but they only bring confusion, guilt, or oppression. Like the vine snake, the devil wants to pluck out our spiritual eyes and blind us to truth.

How should we respond? We can learn from the story of Jesus in the wilderness. The devil tempted Jesus in many ways and even misused Scripture to try to deceive. But Jesus resisted by talking back to the devil.

"Jesus said to him, 'Away from me, Satan! For it is written:
'"Worship the Lord your God, and serve him only.'" Then the
devil left him, and angels came and attended him"
(Matthew 4:10-11).

Speaking to the devil may sound a bit strange but don't worry—we're not suggesting having conversations with evil spirits! Rather, simply by speaking the truth firmly we can take authority over oppressive thoughts.

For example, we may have thoughts like "I'm not good enough to be a Christian." Well, that's true. Nobody's good enough on their own merit. But it is only half the truth. We can respond by declaring, "I know my sin is great but God's grace is greater. Through the death of Jesus on the cross, He has fully forgiven me and accepted me."

In his book, *I Talk Back to the Devil*, A. W. Tozer gives advice for those experiencing condemning thoughts:

Are you still afraid of your past sins? God knows that sin is a terrible thing—and the devil knows it too. So he follows us around, and as long as we will permit it, he will taunt us about our past sins.

As for myself, I have learned to talk back to him on this score. I say, "Yes, Devil, sin is terrible—but I remind you that I got it from you! And I remind you, Devil, that everything good— forgiveness and cleansing and blessing—everything that is good I have freely received from Jesus Christ!"[9]

Do you ever think negative thoughts about yourself and your worth? You may be listening to the vine snake, rather than the true vine. Take hold of God's truth.

Don't allow yourself to be deceived into thinking negatively about yourself. Talk back to the devil and declare how God sees you instead.

Reflect and Respond

Are there things from your past that still trouble your conscience?

Perhaps pray something like this:

Father, thank you that in Christ there is no condemnation for me. Thank you that my sins are wiped out. Thank you that the blood of Christ makes my conscience clean. Thank you for the refreshment that brings.

And don't be afraid to defy Satan's lies:

Satan, I reject your accusations in Jesus' name. I am a forgiven child of God. The Lord has forgiven my sin. Romans 8:1 says there is now no condemnation for those who are in Christ Jesus.

Remember Your Authority

How selfish! I thought, Borrowing a library book and not returning it on time!

I needed to borrow a vital book to prepare for an exam.

Unfortunately, when I visited the library, the book wasn't there. Someone had borrowed it and hadn't returned it. I checked several times over the next few days, but there was no sign of it. The date for returning the book had passed.

I had to take the exam without it. I felt angry because I could have achieved a much better grade if only I'd had the opportunity to read this important book.

One morning, a few days after the exam, I was lying in bed, slowly waking up. As I opened my eyes, I looked up at my bookshelf. And there it was—the book I'd been looking for! I'd borrowed it from the library, but I'd forgotten all about it.

Jesus has given us authority over all the power of the enemy. But if we forget that we have this authority, it's of no use to us. We miss out. We end up putting up with things in our lives that we don't have to.

Spiritual authority is mysterious. We know that all authority in heaven and earth has been given to Jesus (Matthew 28:18). However, he delegates authority to his followers.

In Luke 10, the disciples are excited to discover their authority.

"The seventy-two returned with joy and said, 'Lord, even the demons submit to us in your name.'

He replied, 'I saw Satan fall like lightning from heaven. I have given you authority to trample on snakes and scorpions and to overcome all the power of the enemy; nothing will harm you'" (Luke 10:17-19).

We have more authority than we often realise. Let's not forget the authority Jesus has given us. Exercising godly authority over our minds is key to being free.

Reflect and Respond

How do you feel about the idea that you have spiritual authority?

Use your authority to protect your mind with words such as: I reject that thought in Jesus' name. I close the door to any intrusive thoughts. Instead, I welcome the Holy Spirit to fill my mind with truth.

Day 18

Already Free

Imagine.

You're in a dark prison. Your wrists and ankles are in chains, and the iron door is shut. A guard points a gun at you and threatens to shoot if you try to escape. You feel trapped and defeated. There's no way out, and it's pointless trying.

One day you receive a note. It's from your father.

My Child,

Why do you stay in darkness?

The chains are made of paper. The prison door is unlocked. The guard's weapon is only an imitation.

Get up, walk out, and be free.

From your loving Father

The guard discovers the note and tells you it's not true. He reminds you repeatedly you can't get out. The chains are too strong, the door is locked, and he will shoot you if you try to escape.

What do you do? Do you accept what the guard says or believe the message from your father?

Many of us face that situation. We feel bound up, but the Bible—a message from our Father—tells us we're free.

The apostle Paul reminded the Galatians that Christ *has* set them free. But then he warns them—although they *are* free, they can end up living as though they're *not*. They were in danger of living as slaves even though they weren't.

> "It is for freedom that Christ has set us free. Stand firm,
> then, and do not let yourselves be burdened again by a
> yoke of slavery"
> (Galatians 5:1).

For the Galatians, the slavery was legalism and the pressure and guilt that went along with it. For us, it may be a different kind of slavery. We may feel bound up with regret, fear, feelings of failure, jealousy, resentment, insecurities, or past hurts. What is it for you?

Getting free is easier than you think. Jesus has defeated the spiritual powers and authorities that controlled us.

"And having disarmed the powers and authorities, he made a public spectacle of them, triumphing over them by the cross" (Colossians 2:15).

Those spiritual powers try to influence us with lies and reminders of bad experiences. They intimidate and try to stop us from enjoying the freedom that Jesus has for us. We need to decide whom to believe.

Reflect and Respond

What do those chains represent for you? Write down any thoughts that come to mind.

Perhaps pray something like this:

Father, thank you that Jesus has set me free. Thank you that Jesus has disarmed the spiritual powers and authorities at the cross. Forgive me that I don't always live in that freedom. Please show me any ways that I've allowed myself to be intimidated by the devil. Help me to remove the chains and walk free.

Now imagine the end of the story . . .

As you tug at the chains, you discover that the paper breaks easily. The guard threatens to shoot, but his toy gun only fires blanks. As you walk past the guard, he lunges at you. But he can't reach you because, in fact, he is the one who's bound up with *real* chains. You push the prison door, and it opens easily. With the guard shouting louder and louder, you step out into the light. Free at last.

Why not act out the above scene?

Take the chains off as you say, for example:

Thank you, Jesus, for the victory of the cross. I take off the chains of [whatever it may be]. I walk free from the dark prison, and I choose to live in the light of God's joy and peace.

Then get up and walk out of the room as a way of representing your freedom.

Day 19

Rest – a Gift from God

Walking down a busy street, I heard a screeching sound behind me. I looked around to see a car straining along with a flat tyre. The driver was obviously in a hurry and didn't have time to stop. His determination to keep going was damaging the wheels.

I reflected on how reckless and irrational he was. He just needed to stop for twenty minutes to change the tyre. Then he could go faster and further. The journey would be more comfortable too.

Then I realised something. "I am that driver."

My life was busy, and I was always in a hurry. Everything I did seemed important, and I didn't have time to stop. Feeling worn out and overwhelmed, I was in danger of causing myself damage.

I didn't need more prayer or more Bible reading, or even more faith. I needed to rest.

Some believe we don't need rest because God gives us strength. A leader in the Welsh Revival, Evan Roberts, once thought that. His friends urged him to rest, or he would wear himself out.

He responded: "Tired? Not once. God has made me strong and manly. I can face thousands. My body is full of electricity day and night and I have no sleep before I am back in meetings again."[10]

This confidence may sound spiritual, but sadly, Evan Roberts had two mental breakdowns and his ministry was cut short.

A different revivalist, Charles Finney, approached ministry differently. He said, "No revival can last if the workers do not learn to rest."

No matter how spiritual we think we are, rest is vital. Even Jesus got tired (John 4:6).

Fruitfulness comes when we live God's way. Jesus reminds us that regular rest is a gift from God. [Jesus] said to them,

"The Sabbath was made for man, not man for the Sabbath"
(Mark 2:27).

We need rest, not just for our bodies but also for our souls and our minds.

We're free from legalistic demands often associated with the Sabbath, but we must prioritise regular rest to remain spiritually and mentally healthy.

When we rest from work, we can work from rest. Our work and ministry become more fruitful because we can draw from a deep inner well of joy, peace, and an awareness of God's presence.

Reflect and Respond

To what extent do you prioritise regular rest? How do you rest?

Set aside a time during your working day to be quiet with God.

How can you build regular rest days into your week?

Consider going on a quiet retreat once a year. For example, many monasteries welcome guests to stay.

Day 20

God Wastes Nothing

"[God] says: 'It is too small a thing for you to be my servant to restore the tribes of Jacob and bring back those of Israel I have kept. I will also make you a light for the Gentiles, that my salvation may reach to the ends of the earth'"
(Isaiah 49:6).

When we first saw the pond in the garden of our rented house, we were horrified. The water was stagnant, dirty, and covered in several years' worth of fallen leaves. It was ugly, and we didn't want it.

When Dave and Julie saw it, their response was very different. Being ecologists, they saw what the pond could become and kindly offered to clean it for us. They waded in and began to clear out the mess that had built up over many years.

Dave showed me a handful of the decomposed leaves he'd taken from the pond as they were cleaning it. "That's good stuff," he said. "It's peat. You can spread it in your garden."

I was surprised that the mess had any purpose. I'd planned to dispose of it. However, we implemented his advice. We took a rake, spread the peat over a patch of soil, and sowed some grass seeds. Within a few weeks, a new lawn covered the land.

The peat acted as a fertiliser. It improved the health of the soil and helped the lifeless land to become a luscious green lawn.

God takes the mess in our lives and uses it for our good and the good of others. He wastes nothing. The parts of our lives that we see as worthless—the mistakes, disappointments, and hurts—God uses all of it for his purposes.

As Paul Scazerro said: "God never discards any of our past for his future when we surrender ourselves to him. He is the Lord! Every mistake, sin, and detour we take in the journey of life is taken by *God and becomes his gift for a future of blessing when we surrender ourselves to him*"[11] (emphasis added).

Restoration is God's plan for you. But on its own, it's too small a thing. God will do much more than that. He will make you a blessing to others.

Reflect and Respond

What aspects of your past trouble you the most? Take some time to give those things to God and thank him that he will turn those things to good.

Perhaps pray along these lines:

Thank you, God, that you are my restorer. You heal my mind and my soul. But you do more than that. Thank you for taking the mess [name some of the mess] and turning it for good. You turn it into a blessing. You turn all things to good.

Day 21

Putting It into Practice

It was Sunday morning, and Mr. and Mrs. Duck were getting ready to go to church.

They waddled out of the house, waddled down the street, and waddled into the church. They waddled to their seats and sat down. From there, they looked around and saw lots of other ducks waddling in.

At 11:00 a.m., the duck preacher waddled to the front, waddled up to the pulpit, and began to preach.

"*You* can fly!" he said.

Ooh! thought Mr. and Mrs. Duck, *We can fly!*

The duck preacher continued, "You *can* fly!"

The ducks nodded and quacked in agreement.

Finally, the duck preacher declared, "You can *fly*!"

All the ducks began jumping up and down with excitement. "We can fly! We can fly!" they shouted.

Then the service ended, and they all waddled home.

As you've read this devotional, we hope that you've been inspired, challenged, and excited about what you've read. But on its own, that's not enough. You need to put what you've learned into practice.

Jesus understood the danger that his hearers might enjoy his message but not do anything about it. He told them:

"Therefore everyone who hears these words of mine and puts them into practice is like a wise man who built his house on the rock. The rain came down, the streams rose, and the winds blew and beat against that house; yet it did not fall, because it had its foundation on the rock. But everyone who hears these words of mine and does not put them into practice is like a foolish man who built his house on sand. The rain came down, the streams rose, and the winds blew and beat against that house, and it fell with a great crash" (Matthew 7:24-27).

Both the wise man and the foolish man heard the words of Jesus. The only difference between them is that the wise man put those words into practice. The foolish man did not.

James makes the point with a different word picture:

"Do not merely listen to the word, and so deceive yourselves. Do what it says. Anyone who listens to the word but does not do what it says is like someone who looks at his face in a mirror and, after looking at himself, goes away and immediately forgets what he looks like. But whoever looks intently into the perfect law that gives freedom, and continues in it—not forgetting what they have heard, but doing it—they will be blessed in what they do"
(James 1:22-25).

Continue to apply the steps you've learnt, and let this be the start of a new season in your Christian life as you walk in the freedom, joy, and peace of a healthy mind.

Reflect and Respond

Take some time to look back at the notes you've made in your journal over the last twenty-one days.

Are there any Scriptures or devotions that particularly spoke to you? How can you continue to apply them to your life?

Perhaps finish with this prayer:

Father, thank you for all you've taught me and reminded me of over the last twenty-one days. I want to hold on to it and continue to apply it in my life. Let your Holy Spirit continue to teach me and remind me of everything I need to know so that I can put it into practice. Thank you that you will continue to transform me through the renewal of my mind.

Please help us to improve

We hope you've enjoyed this devotional.

We appreciate your feedback, and we'd love to know your thoughts.

We need your input to make the next version better.

Please leave a helpful review on Amazon.

Thanks so much.

Andrew and Lesley Crisp

Endnotes

[1] Paraphrased from an article on the BBC News Website by Laurence Cawley and Amelia Reynolds: "King's Lynn: The community shop with a chair for those who "are not OK" ", BBC News, July 01, 2021, https://www.bbc.co.uk/news/uk-england-norfolk-57496557.

[2] Lewis B. Smedes, *Forgive and Forget: Healing the Hurts We Don't Deserve*; HarperSanFrancisco, 2nd Revised Edition (2007).

[3] Edwin Othello Excell, Johnson Oatman, Jr., "Count Your Blessings" lyrics © Word Music, LLC.

[4] Andrew K. Przybylski, et al: Motivational, emotional, and behavioral correlates to fear of missing out, cited in *Computers in Human Behavior* Volume 29, Issue 4, July 2013, pages 1841-1848.

[5] David Martyn Lloyd Jones, *Spiritual Depression: Its Causes and Cures;* Zondervan; 2nd Revised Edition (2016).

[6] C. S. Lewis, *Screwtape Letters: Letters from a Senior to a Junior Devil* (C. Lewis Signature Classic); Collins (1 April 2012).

[7] Quoted from a 1960 revised edition of C.S. Lewis, *Screwtape Letters* in an article by John A. Murray: "C.S. Lewis and the Devil", *The Wall Street Journal*, August 05, 2011, https://www.wsj.com/articles/SB10001424053111903454504576486441729097076

[8] Lewis, *Screwtape Letters*.

[9] A. W. Tozer, (2008-09-11T23:58:59). *I Talk Back to the Devil* (The Tozer Pulpit) (Chicago: Moody Publishers; Kindle Edition, [year]).

[10] Quoted in Roberts Liardon, *God's Generals, Why They Succeeded and Why Some Failed* (Whitaker House, US, 2009).

[11] Peter Scazzero, *Emotionally Healthy Spirituality Day by Day* (Zondervan; Reprint edition, 6 Sept. 2018).